# This Little Light of Mine

## Letting Your Light Shine Through Unexpected Acts of Kindness

HONOR
BOOKS

Honor Books
P.O. Box 55388
Tulsa, Oklahoma 74155

*This Little Light of Mine*
*Letting Your Light Shine Through Unexpected Acts of Kindness*
ISBN 1-56292-151-7
Copyright © 1995 by Honor Books
P.O. Box 55388
Tulsa, Oklahoma, 74155

Published by Honor Books
P.O. Box 55388
Tulsa, Oklahoma, 74155

In one of the most famous speeches of all time Jesus told an audience, "You are the light of the world. A city that is set on a hill cannot be hidden. Nor do they light a lamp and put it under a basket, but on a lampstand, and it gives light to all who are in the house. Let your light so shine before men, that they may see your good works and glorify your Father in heaven." (Matthew 5:14-16 NKJV)

A lamp in Bible times was only a few inches long. It was made of clay, filled with olive oil, and lighted by a rag wick. The amount of light that came from such a lamp was no more than that put out by a candle.

A *little* light. Yet worthy to shine on a lampstand. A *little* act of kindness. Something every person can do. Spreading hope, showing love, sharing faith, and giving joy in small ways. In ordinary places. Through simple means. Very often it's the unexpected word, the gentle brief touch, the seemingly insignificant gesture, or the inexpensive gift that makes a wonderful difference in the life of a person who is struggling with emotional pain, depression or illness without hope. You can be a person today who chooses to let your inner light of love and goodwill shine brightly to those around you giving hope to family and friends, and to those with whom you have daily contact in your community, at work or school. The stories and examples offered in this book are illustrations of a "little light" being shown to others. They are all actions that any one of us might take, or have taken.

Don't let anybody keep you from letting your light shine by discounting or ridiculing your expressions of love. Don't let anybody put out your light with hateful words by letting a bushel basket of rejection cover up your glow.

You have something to give. And the world around you desperately needs it!

Why don't you make your motto those final words of the little chorus, *This Little Light of Mine*, that you may have learned as a child — and sing them in your heart with gusto today? Let it shine . . . Let it shine . . . Let it shine!

# *Letting Your Light Shine Before...*

## FAMILY
## AND
## FRIENDS

Tammi jumped when the phone rang. She was alone in the house babysitting her younger brother Jerry and younger sister Kimmy for the first time. At age 14, Tammi had *thought* she was old enough to babysit on her own. After all, some of the babysitters her parents had hired in the past year were only fifteen. It wasn't until her parents left for their dinner party that panic set in. What if something bad happened? What if her brother or sister had an accident. What if they became ill?

To Tammi's great relief, the voice on the other end of the phone was Mom's. "Just checking in honey," Mom said cheerfully. "How are you doing?" Tammi could hardly keep back her tears of relief and managed to say, "Fine, Mom," then added, "When did you say you were coming home?" Sensing Tammi's fear, Mom responded, "We'll be home by ten o'clock. I know you're going to do just fine, Tammi, but I'm a little nervous — after all, this is *my* first time as a mom to be away from all three of you while you are alone. Would it be alright with you if I call every half hour until 9:30 to help my nerves?" "Sure!" Tammi said in guarded relief. "That would be fine."

The rest of the evening went well and Tammi was able to relax. In fact, by the time she received Mom's 9 p.m. call, she had both of her siblings tucked into bed and was calmly reading a book. "You don't *have* to call at 9:30 unless you really *need to*, Mom," she said. "In fact, if you and Dad would like to stay out until 10:30, it's OK with me."

Be there when your children need you, even if they don't *think* they need you until *after* you aren't present.

*How often would I have gathered thy children together, as a hen doth gather her brood under her wings.* — Luke 13:34 (KJV)

The annual Miller Family Reunion was a big deal. Aunts, uncles, and cousins came from five states for three days of cookouts, games and sports. And no one enjoyed it more than 14-year-old Pete Miller. Pete was a natural athlete and loved playing team sports. But his 10-year-old sister Maggie was another story. Tall for her age and uncoordinated, Maggie felt awkward on the playing field.

On Saturday afternoon, all the cousins gathered to play soccer, that is except for Maggie. Pete went looking for her. "Maggie, come on! It's game time!" he said. "I can't," Maggie said, fighting back her tears. "I'm no good. I'm too stupid to do anything."

That's not true!" Pete responded while putting his arm around his big little sister's shoulder. "You beat us all at Scrabble. And that brownie recipe you invented makes the best brownies I ever tasted."

"Those aren't sports!" Maggie sobbed back. "So? You know, you don't have to be a good athlete," Pete gently said. "Sports are just one part of life. Do what you're good at Maggie, but go ahead and have fun with the stuff you're not good at too. Soccer isn't brain surgery! Who cares who wins?"

"You really mean that?" Maggie asked.

"Sure! What matters is doing your best and having fun." Maggie found her smile again and followed her brother onto the field. If Pete thought she was worth having on the team, maybe she could learn to kick that soccer ball after all.

Encourage a sibling to celebrate her talents. Then, show her ways to enjoy activities where she's not a "natural."

*We have different gifts, according to the grace given us...* —Romans 12:6 (NIV)

"**I**'m at the end of my rope!" Rita moaned.

Even from 1,000 miles away, Paul could feel her pain coming through the phone lines. His old college "study buddy" was in trouble. "Tell me what's wrong," he said encouragingly.

"Bruce was laid off last week," Rita said. "That computer company turned out to be less stable than we thought. I've been looking for a job since the twins started school last month. But so far, no good; I'm either over — or underqualified."

"You'll find something," Paul assured her.

"We spent our savings to fix the car, and now there's nothing to fall back on. No health insurance, no —"

"Whom do you trust?" Paul interrupted.

"Excuse me?" Rita asked.

"Are you trusting Bruce, yourself, your bank account — or Someone else?" Paul asked. There was silence on the other end.

"You're right," Rita finally said. "I've been so down, I guess I haven't looked up."

"I know things are tough, but you can't lose hope!" Paul encouraged his old friend. "You need to pray—and so will I. I'll make some calls, too."

Two weeks later, Bruce had a lead on a new job (from a totally unexpected source). The salary was lower, but Rita's spirits were higher. She had forgotten how good it was to put her trust in God.

Do something constructive to help a friend...and don't forget to pray with and for them.

*I long to see you so that I may impart to you some spiritual gift to make you strong — that is, that you and I may be mutually encouraged by each other's faith.* — Romans 1:11,12 (NIV)

"**Y**ou don't need to do this," Carl said. "It's no big deal," Roger replied. "I'd rather have someone to travel with, too." With that, Roger cancelled the last day of his trip so he could fly home on the same plane with Carl. As it turned out, Carl was glad for the company. It was good to have someone to talk to on the fourteen-hour flight. And it was especially good to have Roger's help in explaining a couple of his purchases to the customs agent.

"You don't need to do this," Carl protested. "It's no big deal," Roger said. "Actually, I'm tired of flying. It will feel good to be on the road. I've got some calls I can make if I travel by car." With that, Roger cancelled his commuter flight and drove with Carl for two and a half hours over the mountain roads to Carl's home city. As it turned out, Carl was grateful. Roger's presence helped him stay awake and alert on the road. And his stories kept Carl's mind off the situation that lay ahead.

"You don't need to do this," Carl insisted. "It's no big deal," Roger said. "Besides, I'd like to see your dad, too." With that, Roger went with Carl to the bedside of Carl's father who was facing heart surgery the next morning. Carl was grateful for Roger's strong word of prayer with his father.

"You don't need to do this," Carl said softly, almost in disbelief at the sight of Roger standing in the doorway. "It's no big deal," Roger said with a strong handshake. "I don't have anything else scheduled this morning." With that, Roger handed Carl a hot cup of coffee and sat down next to him in the waiting room until the heart surgeon came out four hours later with a good report.

"Thanks," Carl said as he walked away from the hospital with his friend. Then he added, "And please don't say, 'It's no big deal.'" Roger smiled and replied, "Okay, I won't, if you promise not to say, 'You don't need to do this again.'"

Just "being there" is sometimes the very best thing you can do.

*Comfort those who are frightened; take tender care of those who are weak.* — 1 Thessalonians 5:14 (TLB)

When Katie's father was diagnosed with cancer, she was shocked, but optimistic. After all, medical science had come a long way. But since her dad hadn't seen a doctor soon enough, his cancer had spread. The prognosis was grim. Katie's mother kept her adult daughter up-dated over the phone every day, reassuring her that Dad was coping. Katie agreed that she should plan a nice long visit. But, she didn't feel the need to desert her husband, Rick, to move home to help Dad out.

By the time Katie arrived home for her visit, she was saddened to see that her father had already lost so much weight. He was almost too weak to get out of bed. The brief round of chemotherapy treatments had affected his ability to keep food down. And he required constant care. "Mom, you should hire a nurse," Katie said one morning during breakfast. "You said that Dad's insurance will cover everything, so just call the hospital and . . . "

"Katie, I can take care of him," her mom said calmly while sipping her coffee. "It's no trouble."

"No trouble? Mom, he's—he's so weak! It's going to be such a drain on you! And he gets so irritable sometimes. He said himself that you should hire someone!"

"Katie, the nurses at the hospital taught me how to care for him. And the doctor is only a phone call away. I'm not trying for sainthood; I'm doing this because I love him and because we need each other. There's nowhere else I'd rather be right now. Whatever happens, I'm just so glad I can do this to show him how much I love him!"

"I hope Rick loves me like this," Katie said softly. "Because I think this kind of love is the greatest thing on earth."

If you are physically and emotionally able, help take care of a loved one who is sick.

*Love is very patient and kind. . . . If you love someone you will be loyal to him no matter the cost.* — 1 Corinthians 13:4,7 (TLB)

*Plant a flower bed in honor of each of your children. Keep bouquets of cut flowers from the planting in your child's room as long as the flowers bloom.*

Billy and Kay could hardly believe what they had just heard. *Mom and Dad were going to let them explore the amusement park all morning by themselves?* It was almost too good to be true. Why, that meant they could move through the park as fast as they wanted . . . from ride-to-ride-to-ride. It meant they could ride whatever rides they wanted — in whatever order — and as many times as they liked. What freedom!

The only stipulations were that they were to stay together and were to meet at the central plaza at 12 noon — sharp! Billy and Kay synchronized their watches with Dad, and off they went. What a morning they had! They even arrived at the plaza a few minutes before noon, glad for a little rest. "Do you think we should tell Mom about that creepy guy that followed us for awhile?" Billy asked. "No," said Kay, "let's not worry her."

"Do you think I should admit to Dad that I left one of the souvenirs I bought on that next to the last ride?" Kay suggested. "Naw," said Billy. "I wouldn't."

"I can't believe they let us have all morning to explore on our own," Billy sighed. "Yeah," said Kay. "I guess they must think we're pretty grown up."

About that time, Mom and Dad showed up. "Did you guys have fun?" Mom asked. "Lots!" Kay said. "You'll never believe it," Dad said, holding up a little sack. "Your Mom and I went on this one ride and somebody had left this behind in the car. It's pretty cool." "That was mine!" Kay shrieked. "I left it there. I can't believe you found it!"

"Did you see a creepy looking guy over in that one area of the park?" Mom asked. Billy said, "Yeah, we saw him. He was weird, but we ignored him."

It wasn't until ten years later that Billy and Kay found out Mom and Dad had been there all the time — just a few yards away, out of sight, having the time of their lives as they watched their children having the time of *their* lives!

Giving others freedom to succeed does not mean giving encouragement to fail. Watch over others as you want your Heavenly Father to watch over you!

*Obey your leaders, and submit to them; for they keep watch over your souls, as those who will give an acount. Let them do this with joy and not with grief, for this would be unprofitable for you.* — Hebrews 13:17 (NASB)

*Create a home-made valentine, birthday, or get-well card for an elderly parent — just like you did when you were a child.*

Alex was heading out of town on an assignment for the newspaper he worked for. Actually, he was looking forward to being away from the office and from his hectic family schedule.

The family farewell had not gone very well before he left. Alex's wife, Deanne, was worrying about handling all the family responsibly while he was away, and Alex was too busy to notice her distress.

In the midst of all the chaos, eight-year-old Matthew asked his father if he would be back to hear his class concert on Thursday evening. Alex replied, "Sorry, I'll be out of town."

He said good-bye quickly and walked out the door.

The out of town assignment would take Alex and the newspaper photographer to the Columbia Gorge on the Columbia River. As they approached the canyon, Alex noticed all the windsurfers and the sailboarders. It looked like the ideal life. Carefree. Worry-free. Responsibility-free. Alex wondered where he had gone wrong — how had he missed this good life?

As he sat in his motel room the last night of the assignment, Alex had a sense of emptiness, of not belonging. Not at home, not here, not anywhere. Things that had seemed important to him — God, marriage, children, work — were now slipping away from him.

Then, Alex noticed in his suitcase a greeting card tucked beneath some clothes. The card was from Deanne. It said, "I'll love you till the cows come home." He looked at the card and Deanne's familiar handwriting and melted inside. In that instant, Alex knew exactly where he belonged.

The next day after a long news-feature interview, and a rushed trip home, Alex raced to Matthew's concert, arriving just in time. As he rushed into the school auditorium to sit down, Deanne jumped up to greet him in elated surprise, then led him to their seats. She had reserved two in the second row, "just in case." When Daniel saw them together as the band marched on stage, he grinned from ear-to-ear and waved wildly to say hello. Alex acknowledged him, stood up, and waved back. Then he turned to Deanne and said, "It sure is good to be home."

Give priority to attending your children's special events to let them know how important they are to you.

*What good will it be for a man if he gains the whole world, yet forfeits his soul?* — Matthew 16:26 (NIV)

Elizabeth Sherrill writes of how she grew up fascinated by her mother's beautiful secretary-style desk. It was a mahogany wonder with a writing leaf that folded down to reveal rows of tiny drawers and cubbyholes. Elizabeth says watching her mother "doing her letters" at the desk was a major influence on her writing career.

But her mother, though full of humor and music, had been raised in a very reserved fashion. And Elizabeth longed for the sort of intimate mother-daughter talks that her mother never really felt comfortable with. As an adult, she made one last attempt to reach her mother by pouring her heart out in a letter. She asked her mother to forgive her for the times when she had been critical of her reserved nature, and asked that she let Elizabeth know in whatever way she chose that she was forgiven.

Months and then years passed without a reply. But Elizabeth came to a peace about accepting her mother on her own terms. For the last 15 years of her mother's life, the relationship was light, affectionate and cheerful.

It was over a year after her mother died that Elizabeth was

painstakingly going through the drawers of the beautiful desk she had always known would someday be hers. Lovingly, she polished each drawer and cubbyhole. Discovering a secret compartment, she found some papers inside. There was a photograph of her father, some family wedding announcements, and a one-page letter that had seemingly been refolded many times.

"Send me a reply," it said, "by any method you choose." Remembering those unusually wonderful years the last 15 years of her mother's life, Elizabeth breathed, "Mother, you always did choose the act that speaks louder than words."

It's sometimes easier to love our parents than to like them, but a lifetime of joy is the reward for doing both.

*Honor your father and mother . . . that it may be well with you, and that you may live long on the earth.*— Ephesians 6:2-3 (NASB)

Tommy had his eye on the blue racer down at the bicycle shop for nine months. He lived with his Mother and two other brothers, and money was rather scarce. But he set his eye to have it, and after praying with his mother, went from house to house asking for odd jobs .

One day the boy went a little further out of his neighborhood than he had ever been. As he approached a shoddy, white, weather-beaten cottage surrounded by a rather junky yard, the front door opened and a thin, elderly man beckoned to him. After Tommy explained his problem, the old man told him of a clean up job in his workshop and of a bike he would trade for it, if he could fix it up.

The shop was a mess with automobile parts and other junk piled ceiling high. But in the center, stood up on its kickstand, was a bicycle that looked incredibly like the blue racer Tommy so desperately desired. The bike had no chain and its ten-speed gear shift was disconnected and taken apart.

It had been given as a birthday gift to the old man's grandson who damaged it in a minor accident, and really didn't want it.

It took Tommy most of the money he had earned and four afternoons (with the man's loving help) to get new parts and fix the blue racer. It took another two weeks to clean out his workshop. But he got the job done, and the bike was his. As he got to know the elderly gentleman and shared the experience with his mother, Tommy also came to know of the power of prayer.

Have you asked God lately to help you with your needs? Have you been asked by Him lately to meet another's needs? Take a good look at some of the things you have in storage. Will you really need them again? Do you know someone who could really use them?

*Ask, and it shall be given to you; seek, and you shall find; knock, and it shall be opened to you.* — Matthew 7:7 (NASB)

Eight inches of wet snow had already fallen on top of the freezing rain. Becky was glad Rick had braved the first snowflakes to dash to the grocery store for emergency supplies. At least they had enough baby formula for their infant son. As the wind picked up and the last rays of light disappeared on the horizon, Becky shivered and turned the thermostat up a few degrees. She had just put her son down for the evening and was setting the table for dinner when everything went dark and quiet.

Becky declared to Rick the obvious, "Oh, no. The electricity is off." "Don't worry," Rick said. "They'll get it up soon. Meantime, we'd better light some candles."

Their candlelight dinner would have been romantic except for Becky's concern about the baby. He would be waking for his late-night bottle soon, and she had no way to warm it. She ran through the list of possible solutions in her mind as she ate. New neighborhood...no relatives living nearby . . . traveling through the icy night . . . it would be perilous. Rick's call to the power company revealed the outage was widespread and that the weather conditions were causing patch jobs to break down almost as soon as they were completed.

As the hours passed, Becky silently prayed. "Please, Lord . . . help me figure out a way to heat his bottle before Daniel awakes." A ringing phone jarred Becky from her prayer. "It's Sadie from down the street," Rick relayed. Sadie from the church they'd just joined! "She says they have a gas stove if we want to cook something or heat a bottle."

Becky visibly relaxed as she breathed a thank-you-Jesus prayer.

## Be the first to welcome a new neighbor and give them your phone number.

*Bear ye one another's burdens, and so fulfill the law of Christ.*
— Galatians 6:2 (NIV)

Horror gripped the heart of the World War I soldier as he saw his lifelong friend fall in battle. Caught in a trench with continuous gunfire whizzing over his head, the soldier asked his Lieutenant if he might go out into the "No Man's Land" between the trenches to bring his fallen comrade back.

"You can go," said the Lieutenant, "but I don't think it will be worth it. Your friend is probably dead and you may throw your own life away." The Lieutenant's words didn't matter, and the soldier went anyway.

Miraculously he managed to reach his friend, hoist him onto his shoulder, and bring him back to their company's trench. As the two of them tumbled in together to the bottom of the trench, the officer checked the wounded soldier, then looked kindly at his friend. "I told you it wouldn't be worth it," he said. "Your friend is dead, and you are mortally wounded."

"It was worth it, though, sir," The soldier said.

"How do you mean, 'worth it'?" Responded the Lieutenant, "Your friend is dead!"

"Yes sir," the private answered. "But it was worth it because when I got to him, he was still alive, and I had the satisfaction of hearing him say, 'Jim, I knew you'd come.'"

Being a true friend is being someone on whom another person may count on in all situations.

*Greater love hath no man than this, that a man lay down his life for his friends.* — John 15:13 (KJV)

Charlie Mason's dog, Rebel, was the neighborhood pest. The half-lab-half-blue-heeler was always on the loose, was a champion digger, and left holes in many gardens, yards and flower beds. He also had a taste for garbage cans. Piles of skattered garbage often greeted Charlie's neighbors as their days began.

It wasn't that Charlie was completely negligent. He kept the dog in a fenced yard. But somehow Rebel would always find a way out.

Because of the complaints and havoc Rebel was causing in the neighborhood, Charlie decided to put him to sleep.

Many of Charlies'neighbors were glad at the news. Still others, were very sad. Rebel was always friendly and loved children, despite his pesky ways.

The evening before Rebel's scheduled dog pound trip, the family was heart sick. Then, the telephone rang. On the other end of the phone was a rancher who had been called and told by a woman about a free half-breed Labrador Retriever that would be excellent on a ranch.

The rancher met Rebel and happily said the two were a perfect match!  He could help him catch the pesky fox that had been raiding his chicken coup and corner those raccoons that had been raiding his corn.

As the family said their good-byes in the drive way, Charlie noticed his neighbor standing across the street in her doorway patting a rolled up newspaper in her hand.  She was grinning from ear to ear.

Charlie motioned to her by pointing at the rancher while shrugging his shoulders, as if to say, "did you place the ad?"  In response to his motions, the kind-hearted lady nodded her head, yes.  Thank you...Charlie said quietly, making sure she saw him say it.

Sometimes an unexpected kind thought or action performed by someone outside of a problem can relieve friends and neighbors in the midst of it.

*Do not be overcome by evil, but overcome evil with good.* — Romans 12:21 (NASB)

John's new home was everything he had ever hoped for. It had the right amount of bedrooms and bathrooms. It was on a corner lot. It even had the yard space he wanted for his children and gardening outdoors. The only thing it didn't have was a fence. So the weekend after they moved in, he began to put one in.

He didn't know exactly where his property line ran along Bob's house next door. And Bob's family had been on vacation since John's family moved in. So his new unknown neighbor wasn't around to consult with concerning the fence. But John was so excited to get on with the job of settling in that he began to build anyway. He considered the mowed grass lines that separated their yards as a good border to build along.

Over the next week, John marked out his borders, dug his post holes and cemented them in, then nailed up a fine cedar fence. But when Bob's family returned the next week, they were shocked by what they saw. John had built three feet over on Bob's property line! In fact, he built it almost directly on top of Bob's underground sprinkler lines.

Bob was understandably upset, but he wasn't the type to get irate. Once the problem was completely discussed between the new neighbors and the property lines were legally pointed out, Bob wisely asked John for his opinion on a solution to be worked out.

John was truly sorry for his building mistake. He offered to tear down the fence or to buy Bob's three feet of land. But moved by his new neighbor's sorrow, John had a better plan. He would buy half the fence, since his underground sprinkler lines could still be reached, and he really didn't use that three feet of yard. After all, it was a fine looking fence. But it only ran along one side of Bob's property line. So the other part of his plan would have John help him build the other three sides of fence. Once their families joined in with the carrying and helping, other projects were brought up. And before the end of the summer, both houses had new patios with new hedges and awnings. Most importantly, though, both families had new best friends.

Seek to turn adverse circumstances around. When at all possible, be at peace with all men. There is friendship to be gained in another's mistakes. Be a forgiving, helpful friend.

*If possible, so far as it depends on you, be at peace with all men.*
– Romans 12:18 (NASB)

# *Family and Friends*
## *Little Unexpected Youches*

Call a brother or sister "out of the blue" to tell them how much you appreciate or admire something they did when you were children.

Send a Mother's Day card to a friend who has lost a child. Add a note acknowledging you know how much they must miss their child on this day and remind them of something special that you remember about their child.

Give an elderly parent or grandparent a large-print Bible for his or her birthday.

Put a note that says "I'm so proud of you!" in your son's or daughter's textbook where they will find it later in the day.

Take out a small picture ad in the local paper to wish a loved one a happy birthday

Write Bible verses on pretty note paper (or buy a box of "precious

# *Family and Friends*
## *Little Unexpected Touches*

promises") and place one under your child's pillow
where he or she will find it each night or in the morning.

While mowing your own lawn, mow the front lawn
of your neighbor's yard who is on vacation.

If you are planning to visit a friend or relative in a nursing home,
call the administrator ahead of time to see if you may bring your
well-behaved dog for the residents to watch, pet, or hold.

Send a "thank-you" note to your parents on the occasion of your
promotion at work. Tell them how much you've appreciated their
upbringing as well as their encouragement and support.

When the plant someone gave you begins to bloom,
call them and thank them again.

Put a note in your spouse's suitcase when he travels to tell him you

# *Family and Friends*
## *Little Unexpected Touches*

miss him and are praying for him.
For a special touch, add a pressed flower.

Do another family member's chores for a day.

On your way home from work, pick up your stay-at-home spouse's
favorite dessert and a movie
for the two of you to enjoy after the kids are in bed.

Bring a bouquet of flowers to your child's recital or
theatrical performance as a love gift to the "performer."

Celebrate your child's or teen's spiritual birthday each year. This
may be the date your child made a personal profession of faith in the
Lord Jesus . . . or the date your child was baptized or confirmed.
Have a special meal. Bake a cake. Give a gift with spiritual
symbolism, such as a cross, Bible, or bookmark with
Christian symbols. Remind your child of Jesus' gift on the Cross and
that *you* know his or her life has eternal meaning.

# *Family and Friends*
## *Little Unexpected Touches*

To welcome your teenager home from a date, turn back the covers of his or her bed and leave a little note on your teenager's pillow, saying, "I'm glad you're home safely. I love you!"

Go to the altar to pray alongside your child.

Greet your child at the airport with a welcome home banner.

Take your child out for a special "Dad-and-me" or "Mom-and-me" day at least once a year. Do something that creates a "just us" memory. Take time to talk, and to listen, to your child's dreams and hopes for the future.

Invite your preteen child to accompany you to what he or she may perceive to be an adult-only dress-up event — such as a special concert, theatrical performance, or a party. Alert your child in advance to special customs or manners that may be required, and introduce him or her to others as if he or she were your very special escort or companion.

# *Family and Friends*
## *Little Unexpected Touches*

Let your child overhear you praying for him often, about very specific needs he or she is facing in life.

Write often to your child when he or she is away from you — whether you are away on business, or your child is away visiting relatives or attending camp. Tuck photos into your letters whenever possible. Let your child know that wherever you are, you are thinking about him!

When you know a family member has had a hard day, draw a bubble bath for that person and invite him or her to enjoy a half hour of peace and luxury!

Start a love circuit at your dinner table with everyone holding hands. A squeeze of the hand passes the love on to the next family member. When you "pass the love" you are letting God's love flow through you.

# *Family and Friends*
## *Little Unexpected Touches*

Declare fifteen minutes of quiet to give the bread winner(s) time to unwind from a day's work when they arrive home at night.

Put gas in your spouse's car when you know she's pressed for time.

Prepare a blessing book for older parents. Have each child make a list of favorite memories in the life of their family. Compile the anecdotes into a book to give as a birthday present.

Encourage loving relationships between siblings by expecting each one to give their *own* Christmas present to each person in the family. This is more fun if the gifts are handmade.

Make sure each family member has an opportunity to pick their favorite activity to do on a camping trip or family vacation.

Learn to say "I love you" in many different languages — even in sign language. And then say it!

# *Family and Friends*
## *Little Unexpected Touches*

During final exam week send a "care" package of snacks, notes of encouragement, and Bible verses to a child who is in college.

At the dinner table at the end of each day share one good thing that happened that day!

When you receive a gift or a favor, always write a thank-you note . . . even if it's just two or three sentences.

When a friend says, "Pray for me," do it — immediately.

Offer to babysit for a friend who has a relative in the hospital.

Write a love letter to your husband and mail it to your home address. Let him pick up the mail the day it arrives.

Agree to throw away something (such as old clothes) your spouse has been begging you to toss out for years.

# *Family and Friends*
## *Little Unexpected Touches*

If you have a bulletin board in your home, decorate it in a special way for your child's birthday. Include cute photos of him, his artwork or poetry, and a special card in the center that is signed by family members and friends.

If a friend is depressed, invite her out for a walk — no talking required. Let her know you just want to be there for her... whatever she needs.

Listen attentively to an older relative or friend tell about interesting life experiences, such as the Depression, World War II, meeting their spouse, or favorite family memories. Having a good listener can brighten an older person's day!

Keep extra umbrellas, hats, gloves, and scarves in your car in case a friend or family member forgets theirs.

# *Letting Your Light Shine At...*

## WORK
## AND
## SCHOOL

Weighing not even one hundred pounds and standing less than five feet tall, twelve-year old Mark took his responsibility as a school crossing guard very seriously. One fall day at his south Chicago elementary school Mark was escorting eleven-year old Wendy across the street. Suddenly, a man driving down the same street, slowed his car, stopped alongside the two and began talking to Wendy.

The man informed Wendy that her mother had been injured and had been taken to the hospital for medical treatment. He then invited the troubled young girl into his car so he could drive her to be with her mom. Mark, however, warned Wendy not to go with the man.

Seeing Mark's resistance, the man drove off and left the two children alone. However, within minutes he returned. This time he got out of his car and ran after Mark. But Mark took chase and out-ran the man who then started running after Wendy. Wendy didn't get away. The man took her by the hair and dragged her to his car as Mark ran after the terrified young girl and her would-be kidnapper. When Mark caught up to them he kicked the man in the groin, knocking him over, and picked Wendy up to escape to safety.

As the two fled, the man grabbed a brick lying on the ground and hurled it at the fleeing children. It glanced off Mark's side but missed Wendy because Mark moved to deflect the blow.

School officials commended Mark for his courageous act on Wendy's behalf. Though he felt proud of himself for his surprising show of bravery, he was embarrassed by all the attention and shied away from the publicity.

Be aware of danger to children. Train your children to know dangerous situations and how to avoid them.

*Take heed that you do not despise one of these little ones, for I say to you that in heaven their angels always see the face of My Father who is in heaven.* — Matthew 18:10 (NIV)

Tom was eager to call his longstanding friend Gene to tell him about a great new business opportunity. Tom stood little to gain personally from the investment opportunity, and he genuinely believed Gene would benefit from the "deal" he had just learned about. But Tom wasn't prepared for Gene's response to his call!

Tom had barely explained to Gene the purpose of his call when Gene began to unload. From Gene's immediate rude and hateful remarks, Tom quickly concluded that someone had badly maligned and misrepresented him to Gene. The falsehood was vile and repulsive to Tom. But he saw no way to defend himself. Especially since Gene was raving on at such a rapid rate, with such pent-up steam and deep personal insults. Tom listened as patiently as he could, feeling not only his own pain, but also sensing the pain that Gene was apparently feeling.

Finally, Gene gave pause and Tom said as calmly as possible, "Gene, I'm sorry if you've been wounded. I don't know right now how I can defend myself or what I can do to set things right with you. But I do know this: you've been my friend for a long time, and I wouldn't purposefully do anything to hurt you. I hope you'll still meet with this man and hear him out. I won't come to the meeting. I'm totally out of the deal and I don't stand to gain anything by it. I just think this could be good for you, but that's up to you to decide. Please meet with him and judge the deal on its own merits for yourself." Then Tom hung up.

Gene did meet with Tom's investment advisor, and as the result of the meeting, made an investment that resulted in several thousand dollars of profit during the next few months. Later when the investment advisor offered Tom a "referral" fee, Tom asked that the fee be added to Gene's profit. When Gene heard about this he called Tom and said, "I think I owe you an apology. Can we meet to see if we can sort things out between us?" The two did meet, got to the root of their misunderstanding, and remain friends to this day.

Sometimes the best thing you can do to help a project or a person is to remove yourself from the picture. At other times it is best to lovingly confront an offended friend or acquaintance to determine the cause of the problem.

*He who covers a transgression seeks love, But he who repeats a matter separates intimate friends.* — Proverbs 17:9 (NASB)

*If therefore you are presenting your offering at the altar, and there remember that your brother has something against you, leave your offering there before the altar, and go your way; first be reconciled to your brother, and then come and present your offering.* — Matthew 5:23,24 (NASB)

*See that no one renders evil for evil to anyone, but always pursue what is good both for yourselves and for all.* — 1 Thessalonians 5:15 (NKJV)

Tonya always knew when her daughter, Mariah, had a test at school: she would wake up with a stomachache. Tonya would drive her to school on those days and give her a much needed pep talk. "You always study hard," she said. "This time you know the material and you can do it!" But Mariah usually froze when the test began, and often earned a poor grade.

So at a PTA meeting, Tonya sought out her daughter's teacher, Mrs. Cooper. "How can I help Mariah do better?" Tonya asked.

"I know she's smart." Mrs. Cooper agreed. "But she needs confidence. When Mariah does something well, she needs praise. She needs to know, deep inside, that she can do the job." That evening when Mariah completed chores at home, Tonya made sure that she thanked and praised her. But her daughter's fear of tests continued.

Early one morning a few weeks later, Mariah came into the kitchen while Tonya was having devotions and praying. "What are you praying for, Mom?" Mariah asked.

"Today," Tonya said, "I need help with a presentation I'm making at work. I know all the statistics; I just don't want to forget them!" Mariah pondered her mother's words throughout the day. She always did her best to prepare for her tests. Maybe she should ask God to help her mother now as she taught her for her own test. She did, and later learned that her mother had a confident, smooth presentation.

When the math teacher handed out test papers a few days later, Mariah froze again. Then she remembered how she prayed for her mother and prayed the same prayer for herself. Gradually, her fingers loosened their grip on the pencil and the knot in her stomach dissolved as she read each problem and realized, *I really do know this stuff.*

By your example, let your child see that preparation and prayer make every task less stressful and more successful.

*If any of you lacks wisdom, he should ask God, who gives generously to all without finding fault, and it will be given to him."* — James 1:5 (NIV)

As Roger prepared for work on Monday morning, he surprised his family by singing. The reason for his unusual happiness was soon made known: "Wilson Sneed is on vacation this week," Roger announced. "I feel as if I am, too!" Roger and Wilson did not get along (to put it mildly).

At the accounting firm that employed them, coworkers called them Hatfield and McCoy. The trouble had started six months earlier, when one of Wilson's clients asked for a new accountant. Roger was chosen. And when he was, Wilson retaliated by making sarcastic remarks during staff meetings. He even began trying to woo away some of Roger's clients. At first Roger ignored the sniping. Then he fought back. Eventually the office began sounding and feeling at times like an armed camp.

Colin, a fellow accountant, knew something had to be done. So he invited Roger and Wilson out to lunch – separately – to let them air their grievances. He also made a point of talking to each man every day. And when staff meetings grew tense, he spoke up and casually turned the conversation in a friendlier direction.

Having laid a lot of groundwork, Colin finally invited both men and their wives to dinner at his house. After the meal, the three men adjourned to the patio. There was a hostile silence surrounding them that soon was broken. Colin pointed out each man's strengths, encouraged them both to put past hurts behind them, then eventually convinced them to make a new start. "I don't like being angry," Roger admitted.

"And who needs an ulcer?" Wilson humorously queried. They all agreed and laughed.

When friends or colleagues are fighting, work with both sides. Try to help them find common ground.

*Blessed are the peacemakers: for they shall be called the children of God.* — Matthew 5:9 (KJV)

*Celebrate employee birthdays with a once-a-month lunch outing. Let employees who have birthdays in that month select the restaurant for the department.*

"What good is a computer without a printer?" Lavonne asked her roommate, Angie. "How am I supposed to print out my papers?"

"The computer lab has a laser printer," Angie said. "I think they charge ten cents a page." Lavonne's 386 computer was a hand-me-down from her older brother, who had just upgraded to a 486. But unfortunately, he had not seen fit to give her a hand-me-down printer. So rather than make innumerable trips to the computer lab, Lavonne decided to save for a printer. Between her savings and part-time waitressing job, she had nearly $900 in three months.

To add to that, as a combination birthday/Christmas gift, Lavonne's parents agreed to give her the extra money needed to pay for a printer. Her brother had been scouring the stores for the best deal and found a printer on sale. But the day before the big purchase, Lavonne entered her dorm room to find Angie in tears. "What's wrong?" she asked.

"I lost my job," Angie said. "I was counting on that money to finish paying my tuition for this semester. And I took out that emergency loan two months ago that is due next week. I just don't have it!"

"How much?" Lavonne asked.

"Never mind," Angie said, forcing a smile. "I'll figure something out."

Lavonne thought about the printer — it was such a good deal! But she thought about her roommate — such a good friend! It wasn't a hard decision. The printer could wait.

Be generous with your time, talents, and resources . . . and make up your mind not to worry about being paid back. You'll be reimbursed in ways you never imagined.

*It is more blessed to give than to receive.* — Acts 20:35 (NIV)

"**Y**ou need to go for that supervisor's job," Manny encouraged his cousin, Joe. "You'd be a good supervisor."

Manny shrugged his shoulders. "You know I can't do it, Joey," he said.

"Why not?" Joe demanded. "The guys all respect you, you've been here as long as anybody, and you really know how to get the job done" Then he said, "look, if I can be a supervisor, you can be one too — an even better one."

Manny remained silent, but Joe didn't give up. "You and Gina could use the money — especially with the baby coming. You know the job. You've never been scared of anything before." Finally, in exasperation, Joe shouted at his older cousin and lifelong friend: "Give me one good reason why you won't go for this job, Manny!"

Manny responded softly, "The reports, Joe. Did you forget the reports?" Joe paused. Manny did have a point. There was a weekly report to write up — not a long form, or very complicated, but a required document. And Manny couldn't write anything other than his name. Joe was the only person in the plant who knew his secret.

"I'll do 'em, Manny," Joe said softly. "You keep track and I'll write 'em up." Manny looked at Joe a little suspiciously. "There's nothing that says you have to write the report, Manny," Joe continued, "only that you have to turn them in and they have to be accurate. I'll write 'em. You sign 'em."

And for thirty-four years that's what Joe did. Nobody ever knew that on Friday afternoons when Joe came to Manny's office, for a half hour of overtime without pay, that Joe was writing Manny's report. Neither did anyone know it was Manny who had gone to work immediately after their immigration so his cousin Joey could attend four years of school. The fact was, as far as the two cousins were concerned, nobody else needed to know.

The most noble acts of friendship are often done in secret.

*Be careful not to do your 'acts of righteousness' before men, to be seen by them. If you do, you will have no reward from your Father in heaven.... But when you give to the needy, do not let your left hand know what your right hand is doing, so that your giving may be in secret. Then your Father, who sees what is done in secret, will reward you.* — Matthew 6:1, 3, 4 (NIV)

"**W**hat in the world is that suppose to be?" Grizzled Kevin's new junior high art teacher, Mr. Hent. "It's suppose to be a sunset, but I guess it's not that good," Kevin responded in anguished defense. "I suppose you're right," snapped the overbearing teacher while holding Kevin's water color in his hand. "Did you really think I would see that in this? First sketch out your painting, then color it in!"

The teacher was right, of course, but his manner was insensitive and wrong. When Kevin related Mr. Hent's attitude to his parents, they were naturally concerned. "Maybe he's just having problems adjusting to junior high from his last teaching experience at the university," said Kevin's Dad. "Let's give the man a chance."

But Mr. Hent got steadily worse. Over the next couple of weeks he humiliated several students in front of the class.

"Artists must have a thick skin to take other's criticism if they are to go forward in the arts!" was his lectured purpose for such critique.

So Kevin's Dad gave him a call. Surprisingly, the teacher was moved and encouraged by the man's concerned words.

Over the next three weeks Mr. Hent improved dramatically in his "desk-side" manner. Nevertheless, five parents at the year's first PTA meeting demanded that he be fired. The teacher had embarrassed their children the first week of school, but none had sought him out. After Kevin's Dad stood up for him and Mr. Hent spoke up himself, the parents agreed to work with him, and he stayed on the job. In fact he stayed on so long that twenty-eight of his students went on to college as art majors, and seventeen went to art institutes. By the time of his retirement he had placed teachers and commercial artists, literally, around the world. And none of it would have happened, if not for Kevin's dad's kind words.

Be kind toward other's short comings and assist them to develop and grow. No one is above our loving concern. You never know, your kindness could touch the world.

*Let your forbearing spirit be known to all men. The Lord is near.*
— Philippians 4:5 (NASB)

Maria was staying late in her Florida government office to study some new federal and state regulations when the phone rang. A frantic voice on the other end of the line told her he was calling from Georgia in the hope of transferring his sick father and brother from Florida to a nursing home near him. He said if he could not do this immediately, the space in the nursing home would be offered to someone else. But miles of state and federal red tape stood in his way.

"I'm sorry," Maria said, "but I doubt if anything can be done that quickly."

Then suddenly she remembered something her pastor had said during a church class the previous evening. He related a heartbreaking story about a mother and daughter who recently died. Not long after, the father and one of two sons both began to manifest a degenerative disorder and only the second son remained healthy. Maria asked a few questions, and to her astonishment, discovered the man on the other end of the phone was the person her pastor had spoken about.

Maria felt a chill of awe. Was this why she'd worked late? Had

God placed her here so she could help this young man with her special knowledge of these laws? "I'll hand-walk the papers through for you" she replied. Thanks to Maria's efforts, the case was concluded in time for the father and son to be moved together.

"Before that evening," says Maria, "my job had seemed more frustrating than fulfilling, and I'd been praying for ways to better serve the Lord with my life. But after helping that Florida family, I began to see the proof of something my husband had said to me: "We can be used wherever we are.""

**If you will think of your work as a ministry, you will become the minister God means for you to be.**

*If we live in the Spirit, let us also walk in the Spirit.* — Galatians 5:25 (NIV)

Even without the torn jeans, he made a scruffy-looking ten-year-old. His fifth-grade classmates had never seen anyone as poorly dressed and unpolished as Marco. This was his first day of elementary school in a quaint New England town of well-to-do families. Marco's parents were migrant fruit pickers and his classmates eyed him with suspicion for the first part of the day. Even though they whispered and made comments about his clothes, he didn't seem to notice.

Then came recess and the kickball game. Marco led off the first inning with a home run, earning him a bit of respect from his wardrobe critics. Next up to kick was Richard, the least athletic and most overweight child in the class. After his second strike (amid the groans of his classmates), Marco edged up to Richard and quietly said, "Forget them, kid. You can do it!" Richard struck out, but at that precise moment, something began to change in Marco's class. Over the next few months, Marco was able to teach the class many new things. Things such as how to tell when fruit was ripe, how to call a wild turkey, and especially, how to treat other people.

By the time Marco's parents finished their work in the area, the class was preparing to celebrate Christmas. While other students brought the teacher fancy scarves, perfumes, and soaps, Marco stepped to the teacher's desk with a special gift. It was a rock that he delivered into the teacher's hands which was beautiful and bright. "I polished it up special," he said.

Years later, the teacher still had Marco's rock on her desk. At the beginning of each school year, she would tell about the gentle boy who taught her and that year's class of fifth graders to not judge a book by its cover. And that it's what's on the inside of others that truly counts.

Children learn things by example that a thousand words could not help them understand.

*While we have opportunity, let us do good to all men.* — Galatians 6:10 (NASB)

*Bring a single rose in a bud vase to congratulate a friend who's had a birth in the family or some other special event.*

With jobs being scarce in her small town, Florence was glad for her new job at the town's only truck stop. She had just started making the coleslaw one afternoon when a middle-aged man came, put some money on the counter, and asked for a *Playboy* magazine. Florence had straightened the magazine display that morning and knew there weren't any in the rack.

She said, "We don't . . ."

"Sure you do," said the man as he pointed to the sign with the bunny logo."

Florence replied, "Well, even if we do, *I* can't sell that stuff."

The customer got enraged and cursed at her. Noticing her dilemma, another waitress came to Florence's rescue and volunteered to get the magazine for the customer. "They should have told you," the waitress said, "there's some more *Playboys* and other "skin" magazines under the counter."

Florence expected to be fired when she told her employer's wife, Della, "I can't work here if I must sell those magazines." Della explained that she didn't like the magazines either and that it was her husband Frank who ordered them. She then told Florence that if a customer asked her for any of these magazines, she would take care of it.

At the midweek church service, Florence asked for prayer saying she didn't know if she should quit the job and that she just wanted to do what was right.

The next week at work Florence noticed that many people were coming into the truck stop solely for the magazines. Not one trucker was among them. It didn't take long to figure out that her employer was providing this smut for his friends. Some were even people she knew from her own neighborhood.

Unable to continue, Florence told Della she could no longer work there because of the conviction she felt for even being around the immoral magazines. Della didn't want to lose her, so she decided to talk to Frank about it. To her surprise Frank said he would remove the current magazines from the store and cancel all future orders. Excited by the news, Della called Florence and gratefully thanked her. "Thank me for what?" Della asked. "For giving me courage to speak to Frank about the magazines."

Stand up for what is right, and you will strengthen others to do the same.

*Be bold and strong!  Banish fear and doubt! For remember, the Lord your God is with you wherever you go.* — Joshua 1:9 (TLB)

"**Y**ou!...the blonde haired girl with the ponytail!" huffed and puffed Miss Hill, her face red from rushing down the length of the hall. She pointed a condemning finger at Joanie, who turned to stare at her accuser with saucer-size eyes.

"Don't try to look so innocent!" Miss Hill bellowed in a loud, angry tone. "You know it is against the rules to run in the hallway! Now I want you to march right back down that hallway and walk back to this classroom while I stand at the doorway and watch!"

Joanie was mortified, and her friend, Jenny knew it. She watched as the color drained from Joanie's face, then watched it return through a flush of embarrassment as tears welled up in Joanie's eyes. *Why didn't she say something?* Jenny angrily thought. Joanie wasn't the one who had run in the hallway. *Why didn't Miss Hill know that?* There were at least five other girls in Jenny's classroom with blonde hair and ponytails. *Why had Miss Hill picked on Joanie?* Joanie was the most shy, timid, girl in the third grade. *Why couldn't Miss Hill see that the real runner had been Edie, who was pretending hard not to know what was happening in the back of the classroom?*

Finally, Jenny spoke up: "It wasn't Joanie who was running, Miss Hill."

"Oh?" Miss Hill responded with a cold glare. "Then just who was it? You?" Jenny didn't say anything. "Very well, Jenny, start walking." Jenny silently walked out of the classroom with all eyes staring at her. She then walked the entire length of the school hallway, to the playground and back, under Miss Hill's accusing eye.

Edie's mocking sneer didn't bother Jenny in the least. Joanie's smile more than made up for it.

## The stronger shoulders are meant for carrying the heavier loads.

*This is my commandment, that you love one another, just as I have loved you. Greater love has no one than this, that one lay down his life for his friends.* — John 15:12,15 (NASB)

*Who is there to harm you if you prove zealous for what is good? But even if you should suffer for the sake of righteousness, you are blessed.* — 1 Peter 3:13-14 (NASB)

Angelo's reputation at the local hardware store was widely known. In fact, he was the reason many people shopped there. One day an 11-year old boy came in and told Angelo all about the go-cart he was going to build. The youngster didn't have a drawing and didn't know how to built it, but it existed in great glory in his mind. When he gave Angelo a detailed description of his dream go-cart — the wheels, the sides, the paint, the driver's seat, and steering wheel — Angelo listened patiently.

"I know exactly what you have in mind," Angelo said once the boy finished his description. He then began gathering items from the store that the would-be go-cart driver would need to build it. He picked out a rod for the axles, the screws, nails, braces that would be needed, then ordered the cart's special wheels.

When they finished, Angelo asked the young boy where he went to school. After the boy told him Angelo said, "Great school. You have to work hard there, don't you? Anyone who goes to that school gets a ten percent discount here at the store."

The name of the school obviously didn't matter. The special discount simply gave Angelo a good reason to reduce the price of the materials to put it within the budget range of the young, would-be go-cart driver.

## Spread kindness through generosity – of heart and material goods – when it is within your ability to do it.

*Each man should give what he has decided in his heart to give, not reluctantly or under compulsion, for God loves a cheerful giver.* — 2 Corinthians 9:7 (NIV)

On the first day of their new job in a fast-paced, New York engineering firm, Paula and her two friends were taken to their work area. It was a large room with several other secretaries. As the new-comers were shown to their work areas, no one smiled and only one person said hello. It was anything but a warm reception for the three women.

Paula thought the behavior was unusual, but rationalized they were probably either too busy or had had a bad day. At lunch, Paula and her friends compared notes. They all had the same reaction. It was now official: their new workplace was very cold and unfriendly with an unusual amount of hostility everywhere.

The following days were similar. With each passing day the three new secretaries grew increasingly aware of how this underlying hostility in the firm made everyone uncomfortable and even got in the way of completing their work. The new secretaries were getting discouraged but they didn't want to quit.

So one day Paula suggested to the others they make a concerted effort to be kind to and to help the other secretaries they encountered on the job. They would continue their work without complaining, then offer to help the others as much as they could in any spare time.

At first they didn't see any results. The complaining and gossip continued. But they didn't give up. About a month after they started their encouraging experiment, one of the older secretaries told Paula she had over-heard one of the engineers give her a rush job. Then she said, "My work is light this morning. Can I help you?" Paula could hardly believe her ears!

Similar incidents began to occur more frequently as the mood in the department gradually began to change. Within six months of Paula and her friends joining the firm, the atmosphere in their office had been definitely changed. It was now marked by smiles, light chatter, and an attitude of helpfulness and cooperation.

Instead of spreading gossip, use the office grapevine to spread words of praise and encouragement about good deeds and accomplishments. When you have the time, go the extra mile to help others with their needs.

*Without wood a fire goes out; without gossip a quarrel dies down.*
— Proverbs 26:20 (NIV)

# Work and School
## Little Unexpected Touches

Pass on news — such as magazine articles or newspaper clippings – that you think could benefit your friends or colleagues in their work or school projects.

Always knock before entering a colleague's work space, even if his or her door is open.

Each week, choose a different colleague as your "secret pal." Do something to honor that person during the week — perhaps by writing an anonymous letter of praise to the person's supervisor. Don't let the person discover your identity!

Invite that person in the cafeteria who doesn't appear to ever have anyone to sit with to join you at your table for lunch.

Clean up your own messes — not only in your own work space, but in the community spaces you share with others.

Refuse to pass on dirty or ethnic jokes, gossip, or unfounded rumors.

# *Work and School*
## *Little Unexpected Touches*

Don't "cut in" in routine lines.

Remember your employees' or colleagues' "anniversary dates" with a thank-you or congratulatory note.

Instead of spreading gossip, use the office grapevine to spread words of praise and encouragement about good deeds and accomplishments.

Let the evening clean-up crew know they are appreciated with a plate of homemade cookies left especially for them in the coffee room.

Develop a buddy system for new employees at work or new children at school to show them around, have lunch together, and introduce to your friends.

Organize a corporate adopt-a-school program for your workplace. Choose a school and offer Saturday tutoring, work tours, part-time employment to students, and perhaps sponsor a school cleanup day.

# *Work and School*
## *Little Unexpected Touches*

Let your children's school teachers know you appreciate their hard work. Send a note of encouragement and thanks when your child comes home with a good report card.

Pack an extra snack in your child's school lunch to share with a friend or with a child who doesn't have one.

Ask a colleague who's having a struggle if you may stop and pray with him when the two of you are alone for a moment. Then say a very short but specific prayer of faith.

Openly and genuinely praise the work of a fellow student or colleague in the presence of others.

Offer to babysit for someone in the office who is a single parent and could use an evening out.

Stay late at work to help a colleague put together a rush project, even if that project isn't your responsibility.

# *Work and School*
## *Little Unexpected Touches*

Offer to do a friend's copying job while you're doing your own.

If you know a fellow student is hurting financially, write an anonymous, caring note and slip it under his door with a $5 or $10 bill (or whatever you can afford) tucked inside.

Bring low-fat or fat-free munchies to work occasionally to share with colleagues during coffee breaks.

If you know a coworker is trying to quit smoking, send him anonymous notes of support and encouragement. Leave packs of gum on his desk.

Running for class office? Vying for a promotion? If you lose, go to the winner and offer your congratulations and support.

Rather than bring your teacher an apple, bring her a student who did his homework and isn't afraid to raise his hand in class: You.

# *Work and School*
## *Little Unexpected Touches*

Make cupcakes instead of a cake for the next office party. It's easier to divide up the leftovers, or share the leftovers with other departments.

When a coworker is stressed out, give him two tickets to a concert or sporting event that you know he would enjoy.

When a valued employee is retiring, make a videotape of each person in the office saying something nice about her, and give her the tape at her retirement party.

If a coworker is getting married and he's strapped for cash, why don't you and several others in the department offer to cook and serve the rehearsal dinner, as a wedding gift from all of you to the happy couple?

Be considerate of your coworkers. Don't pop or crack gum; wear just a touch of perfume and aftershave (a little goes a long way); and watch how loudly you speak. Do unto others.

# Work and School
## Little Unexpected Touches

Be on time for class, meetings, or appointments. It shows that you respect others.

When answering a coworker's phone, be sure to get the name right and the message straight — and ask for a phone number so he can return the call.

If you use the coffee/break room at work, leave it as clean as or cleaner than you found it — whichever is cleaner.

# *Letting Your Light Shine In...*

# YOUR COMMUNITY

For days, Patti watched a frail, little elderly woman arrive each afternoon at 1:45 to sit on a bench across from Patti's New York City apartment building. She stayed for three hours, regardless of weather conditions, staring at the door to Patti's building. Then as if on cue, at precisely 4:45 she would arise and walk back up the street. Moved with curiosity, Patti went down to visit with the woman one afternoon. Taking a seat next to her on the bench, she casually asked, "What are we watching?"

The woman rambled on about how she believed her father lived in the building and that she was hoping to catch a glimpse of him. It didn't take long for Patti to realize that the woman, a street person named Priscilla, was suffering from dementia. So for the next several days, she would take a few minutes to sit with the woman. She shared a thermos of hot cocoa with her, then gave her the thermos. She gave her a warm sweater one day, mittens and a shawl on others. Then one afternoon Patti said, "I don't think your father lives in *this* building, Priscilla. But I think I know where he *does* live. Would you like for me to show you?"

Priscilla agreed, and the two of them walked around the corner to a small church. They sat on a pew in semi-darkness, speaking occasionally about the beauty of the stained glass windows. Then Patti began to talk to Priscilla about her Heavenly Father. The next week, Patti and Priscilla sat for a few minutes each day on the bench below Patti's apartment, then walked together to the church. One day a minister of the church introduced himself to them and gave Patti the opportunity to tell him about meeting Priscilla. To her surprise, Priscilla began telling the minister about her Father . . . her Heavenly Father . . . the One whom she enjoyed coming to visit every day at the church. The minister helped Priscilla find a room with members of his church, where she lived for nearly two years . . . before Priscilla truly went home to see her Father.

**Learn the name of a street person you may see with some regularity. Call that person by name. Pray for that person daily.**

*Inasmuch as ye have done it unto one of the least of these my brethren, ye have done it unto me.* — Matthew 25:40 (KJV)

*On a hot summer day, offer your mail carrier an ice-cold glass of lemonade.*

Nancy was shocked at what she saw when she walked into Mildred's house. It was obvious Mildred hadn't been able to clean her home for some time. Newspapers, partially empty cans of food, magazines, clothes and paper sacks filled with garbage, were strewn about everywhere. A narrow path cutting through a pile up of dirty dishes and trays led from the living area to Mildred's unmade bed.

An odor of gas filled the apartment. Nancy quickly found a burner left blazing on the gas stove in the kitchen that was letting it out. The house's sagging porch, a leak in the corner ceiling of the bedroom, mildew in the bathtub, and the sound of its howling plumbing completed the scene of decay.

Mildred seemed oblivious to the filth around her. But Nancy didn't want to overstep her role as a church visitor to the homebound. Still, Nancy was concerned that if a social worker came calling, Mildred might lose her home against her will.

After breathing a quick prayer for God's wisdom, Nancy said, "Mildred, I know a few teens who are being trained for a special mission to Mexico. They need a place to put in a few hours of on-the-job training in cleaning and repair. Would you be kind enough to let them put in some of those training hours here in your home?" Mildred wasn't all that happy about *receiving* assistance, but she was more than happy to *help* these youngsters out!

So Nancy called the youth group leader at the church, and her team quickly responded. Within two weeks, Mildred's house was clean and restored to good repair. The teens who did the work not only had a sense of satisfaction at a job well done, but they now felt prepared to take on the tasks they would be doing on their missions trip. On top of that, they all had fun working together while building team morale!

## True community service is always a win-win situation.

*Give and it will be given to you; good measure, pressed down, shaken together, running over, they will pour into your lap. For whatever measure you deal out to others, it will be dealt to you in return.* — Luke 6:38 (NASB)

One of Darcy's favorite times of the year was Christmas morning. But one of her *least* favorite times was Christmas afternoon. It seemed to her that the joy and excitement of opening presents on Christmas morning nearly always degenerated into squabbles, exhaustion, and frustration by mid-afternoon. The thrill of new toys quickly vanished and the "giving" spirit rarely extended to a "sharing" spirit among her six children.

Still, Darcy dreamed of seeing her children enjoy Christmas cheer and good will ALL DAY. And she found inspiration to create such a day the Christmas her husband Keith was injured with a broken pelvis. While visiting him in the hospital on Christmas afternoon, Darcy realized Christmas was "just another work day" for hospital personnel, and "just another sick day" for those who were hospitalized. So she came up with a plan.

Starting the next September, she and her children began to make small gifts to take to hospital patients of various ages. They also rehearsed songs, even adding a little choreography to go with some of them. When Darcy contacted the hospital administrator to ask permission to visit and perform for individual patients on Christmas afternoon, he was delighted.

This is how Darcy, Keith, and their six children began their annual Christmas afternoon visits to St. Mary's hospital. For three hours every Christmas they sang and gave their gifts away from room to room, and at nursing stations, spreading the joy of Christmas morning throughout the entire day. For twelve years they kept the family tradition alive...and then...they multiplied their efforts. By that time, several of the children were married and had started families of their own. So they took on *two* hospitals. Half of the family visited St. Mary's and half visited County General in the next town. Then on Christmas Day eve they would all meet for dinner to share highlights of their "Bedside Carols" tours!

The best way to turn a bad time into a joyful time is to start giving.

*God himself is teaching you to love one another. Indeed, your love is already strong toward all the Christian brothers throughout your whole nation. Even so, dear friends, we beg you to love them more and more.* — 1 Thessalonians 4:9, 10 (TLB)

*Letting Your Light Shine In...*
## YOUR COMMUNITY

Louise struggled to keep her family fed after a divorce left she and her children in poverty. For two years the single mother received welfare assistance, but it still required a lot of ingenuity on her part to make ends meet. Part of her plan to stretch the food budget involved the use of vendor coupons. She became so skilled at shopping with coupons that she could now feed her family of five for $25 a week.

When Louise married Kevin, you would think she would have wanted to get as far away as possible from the challenging struggles she had just been through. But, instead of ignoring and forgetting those in need, just as she was, Louise decided to help them. When Louise was on welfare she came to see hungry people in a very different way and she wanted to make a difference.

So not long after the wedding Louise began teaching classes on coupon shopping to welfare recipients and the working poor. Both she and Kevin began to put into practice the principle, "Give a man a fish, feed him for a day; teach a man to fish, feed him for life."

Working together, Louise and Kevin soon put together a network of churches and organizations that collected coupon inserts from the

Sunday papers. A group of inmates at a nearby penitentiary agreed to sort the coupons. And residents of a retirement village agreed to cut them out. The coupons are currently being distributed by Louise and Kevin to different service agencies in order to get them to those in need.

When you are able to get out of dire circumstances, don't forget others who may still be there. Help them to find their way out.

*We love, because He first loved us.* — 1 John 4:19 (NASB)

*The things you have heard me say in the presence of many witnesses entrust to reliable men who will also be qualified to teach others.* — 2 Timothy 2:2 (NIV)

*Help disabled or elderly neighbors with leaf raking and snow shoveling.*

The annual family garage sale had always been a trusty means for the Babcocks to raise some extra money to help pay for a few extras on the family vacation. And this year they had a big ticket item — their daughter's bedroom suite. As Rose looked it over she was sure it would bring in her asking price of $200.

On the morning of the sale, the early-bird customers were gathered to get the best deals. Baby clothes and ties sold quickly and two women were looking closely at the bedroom suite. One of them asked Rose if she would lower the price, but she held firm, confident that she had priced it fairly.

Later that morning a young couple showed some interest in the furniture. The wife was pregnant, her husband had a cast on one arm and their three children were obediently following them from place to place. Rose quickly found out they were looking for furniture to replace what had been vandalized or stolen when their house was broken into a week earlier. They also asked if she could come down on the asking price. This time, Rose deliberated with her husband for a few minutes. She really was counting on that money – perhaps for a whitewater raft ride this year. But Rose reasoned, as always the Babcocks would get their family vacation this year, but this family was looking to replace the basics of life..

Rose returned to the couple and announced her new price. "Free?" the couple asked incredulously. "You mean just take it?"

"Absolutely," Rose responded, and offered a stack of dishes to go on the table as well. Then Bob offered to put a notice in the church newsletter for any other items they might need. The young couple was overwhelmed as customers helped load up the truck with their "new" furnishings. "We love you and Jesus loves you!" Rose said again as the couple drove off.

Share what you have with others. Often you get back far more than the asking price!

*No one claimed that any of his possessions was his own, but they shared everything they had.* — Acts 4:32 (NIV)

When Don came home from work one afternoon, he saw a familiar sight. Mrs. Brinks was slowly getting out of a cab. The driver, a little impatient, was holding two bags of groceries. Don watched the pair make their way to Mrs. Brinks' apartment door. Then the driver trotted out to his cab and squealed his tires to get out of the parking lot.

For some reason, Don couldn't get this scene out of his mind. Mrs. Brinks sort of reminded him of his grandmother. Maybe that was it. In the laundry room the next Saturday, he mentioned Mrs. Brinks to his neighbor, Fran.

"Her husband died last summer," Fran said. "He did all the driving and her kids live 2,000 miles away. She doesn't get out much, I guess."

After hearing this, Don knew he had to do something. So on Sunday afternoon, he and Fran went to the woman's apartment with a loaf of Fran's freshly-baked bread. Once invited in, the two of them said they would love to take turns driving Mrs. Brinks to the grocery store and on other errands. "But I don't want to be a bother!" Mrs.

Brinks said. "It's no bother," Don insisted. "We want to do this," Fran agreed.

A schedule was set up, and the chauffeuring service began. Before long, the three neighbors became good friends, each bringing their own special gifts and talents to the relationship. Everybody won.

Giving doesn't have to involve money. A gift of time and thoughtfulness can be just as valuable.

*This is pure and undefiled religion in the sight of God and Father, to visit orphans and widows in their distress, and to keep oneself unstained by the world.* — James 1:27 (NASB)

*Be devoted to one another in brotherly love; give preference to one another in honor.* — Romans 12:10 (NASB)

The town library had been a popular gathering place for as long as anyone could remember. Aside from its usual mission of checking out books, the library gave people a place to meet friends, discuss local events, and a safe place for children to begin their homework while waiting for parents to pick them up. Understandably, the entire town was up in arms when City Hall announced cutbacks that would allow the library to be open just three days a week, for six hours a day.

"That's preposterous!" said Denise, mother of a seven, a nine, and a thirteen-year-old. "Where will the kids go? And what about the college students and the older people who go in every morning to read the paper and talk to each other?! What is this town coming to?"

"Don't just complain; do something," her husband, Steven, advised. "Volunteer some time to help keep the doors open." *Good idea*, Denise thought, *except I can't do more than a few hours a week. That's not enough.*

Denise's next-door neighbor Ginny suggested they should

recruit a few more volunteers and then go talk to a City Council member. When they did, the councilman wasn't sure a mostly volunteer staff would work, but he pitched the idea at the next meeting. By a narrow margin, the council agreed to a three-month trial run.

The volunteers knew their job wouldn't be easy, but this was a cause worth working for.

## Don't let something you believe in die. One person can make a big difference.

*As the body without the spirit is dead, so faith without deeds is dead.* — James 2:26 (NIV)

In the months leading up to the First Physical Challenge 15K Charity Run, nearly every non-runner in town was asked to be a sponsor. Most were happy to oblige. But Jim had little enthusiasm for the race. A motorcycle accident five years earlier had put him in a wheelchair, and the thought of all those healthy people running through the streets of town was hard to handle. All the same, his wife, Judy, tried to persuade him.

"You don't get it," Jim said. "I feel like I'm invisible when they have these things. They take their legs for granted. They can't imagine what it's like to be in this chair!"

"But you aren't the only one," Judy said. "I can think of five other people who have disabilities. Maybe you need to remind people that you're all really here!"

Moved by Judy's passion, Jim discussed the race with Bill, a Vietnam vet who was also in a wheelchair. "Let's enter the race," Bill said. "Guys like us do this all the time."

When word got out that Jim and Bill were entered in the event, three other disabled people signed up. "They could change the name to the 'Physically Challenged 15K,'" one woman mocked. But after taking time to think about it she continued, "when you think about it, though, most of us find fault with our bodies. Sure, some flaws are more obvious than others. But aren't we all trying to do what we can with what we've got?"

After the race, in which Jim and Bill placed a hard earned thirty-third and thirty-fourth, he told the crowd, "I didn't plan to start a movement." Then he paused... "wait," he said, "I take that back. Now I guess I really do want to start a movement. I think we should all get moving — you people who can walk, as well as we who can't. Let's all do what we can to get into next year's race. I haven't felt this good for years. And let's don't count anyone out, as long as they're alive!"

Never underestimate your ability to influence others. Be a force for good in your neighborhood.

*...The race is not to the swift, nor the battle to the strong,...but time and chance happen to them all.* — Ecclesiastes 9:11 (NKJV)

"Can I invite Laury to my birthday party?" Bonni asked. "Of course," her mother, Lisa, said. "Will she need a ride?" "Yes," said Bonni. "Her mom doesn't have a car." "No problem," said Lisa. "Just get her address." When Bonnie gave her Laury's address, Lisa was surprised to find she lived in low-income housing. Bonni hadn't talked much about her new friend.

The day of the party, Lisa was a little apprehensive as she drove to Laury's project. She never came to this part of town. It was a dangerous place to live.

Laury's mom, Jean, unlatched several locks before letting Lisa in. There were circles under her eyes, deep frown lines on her face, and a mixture of hopelessness and fear in her raspy voice. "Laury's almost ready," she said. "Sorry that she can't bring a gift. My paycheck didn't—"

"It's okay," Lisa said. "It's just a party, just to have fun. Gifts aren't necessary." *Besides, you need your money to survive*, Lisa thought as she looked around the sparsely furnished room. A child was crying in another room. It was Laury's little brother. Jean brought him into the living room. He looked unhappy, too.

"Why don't you both come with us?" Lisa asked on impulse. "A couple of the other mothers will be there too, and I'd like to get to know you better. I bet we have a lot in common." Jean shook her head, "no," but Lisa pressed on. "Please come. I really want you to."

Lisa won the battle of wills and Jean came to the party. Once there Lisa and the other mothers surrounded her with love and she slowly began to warm up. It was the first step in a long journey toward building her own self-esteem, as well as that of her children. After the party Bonni invited the family over for hot dogs and swimming the next Friday night. "Thank you," said Jean tearfully. "Can I bring anything?" "Yes," said Lisa, "you can bring the buns. But most importantly, bring yourselves — we look forward to getting to know you."

A journey begins with a single step. Start with small good deeds and work up to the big ones.

*Offer hospitality to one another without grumbling. Each one should use whatever gift he has received to serve others, faithfully administering God's grace in its various forms.* — 1 Peter 4:9,10 (NIV)

The new playground was a big hit. At long last, neighborhood children had a safe, clean place to play. Parents and babysitters could sit and talk while the children put the equipment to good use.

"If we could only harness their energy . . . " mused Marsha to her friend Peg. Peg laughed. "You said it. I don't know where my Tommy gets his. He never seems to sleep."

"It must be all the fruit drink and cookies," Marsha said. Then as she was watching her daughter Jo at play, Marsha noticed another little girl for the first time. *Haven't seen her around here before,* she thought. The longer she watched, the more concerned she became. Suddenly, a couple of boys bullied the girl off a swing. No adult came to her rescue. *Where is her mom?* Marsha wondered. *Is she here alone? I'd better keep an eye on her.*

It was the same every day for the rest of the week. The girl, Ruby, mostly played alone. Finally, Marsha decided to take action. "Who brings you to the park?" she asked.

"My daddy," Ruby said. "He has to work. He can't stay." Marsha frowned. "Do you have a mommy?"

"She's dead," Ruby said, her chin quivering. Marsha gave her a hug.

"I want to talk to your daddy," Marsha said. "Tell him I'll look out for you. You really shouldn't be here alone." Ruby nodded and went back to the swings. Then Marsha returned to her bench. *I hate interfering in other families' business,* she thought, *but sometimes, for the sake of a child, you have to speak up.*

As it turned out, Ruby's regular babysitter had gone on vacation for two weeks. Unable to find another sitter, Ruby's father had trusted that Ruby would be safe in the community park. After talking with him, Marsha agreed to meet Ruby each morning for the four days remaining before the babysitter's return. She gave only one condition—her father would have to drive Ruby to personally drop her off. Ruby played safely. Marsha didn't worry. And Ruby's father was very grateful!

If you think a child might be in an unsafe situation, speak to the parents and keep your eyes open.

*The Lord will keep you from all harm — he will watch over your life; the Lord will watch over your coming and going both now and forevermore.* — Psalm 121:7,8 (NIV)

"You're out!" the umpire bellowed as Eric slid into home plate. Dejected, Eric brushed himself off and returned to the dugout. He was the third out.

"Tough break," and "good slide," his teammates said. Coach Barnes, his best friend's dad, slapped him on the back. "Keep your chin up," he said. "It ain't over yet."

Two more innings came and went. Then, it was the bottom of the ninth. The Redbirds led by three runs. Eric's team, the Lions, had to win, or they'd be out of the tournament. There were two outs; Eric needed a hit or a walk. But he was too nervous to focus on the ball and swung wildly at the first two pitches.

"Settle down!" Coach Barnes yelled. Eric did, and took the next three balls for a full count. The next pitch, Eric swung with all his might and hit the ball over the left fielder's head. "Run!" the fans screamed. He ran — first, second, third, and was waved home by the third base coach. A homerun!

But something was wrong. The first baseman claimed that Eric had missed the bag. Coach Barnes stood beside the umpire, arms folded, head down. Then, he pulled Eric aside.

"Did you touch the bag?" he asked.

"I don't know," Eric said, red with frustration.

His coach sighed. "I was watching. I don't think you did. We have to tell them."

"But we'll lose!" Eric protested.

"We have to be honest," the coach said. "Can we enjoy the next game if we know we don't belong there?"

"I guess not," Eric said sadly. "We better tell 'em." It hurt, but he knew his coach was right.

When you are in charge, act with integrity. The people on your team need a leader they can trust.

*Train a child in the way he should go: and when he is old, he will not depart from it.* — Proverbs 22:6 (KJV)

After twelve weeks in a recovery group for victims of childhood sexual abuse, Jane felt she had made great progress in dealing with the anger and shame she had felt for many years of her life. She went through each of the steps for recovery, but struggled with the last one — forgiveness for her abusers. This was out of the question. There was no way she could even imagine that.

Several months later while grocery shopping, Jane overheard an elderly man in the store asking shoppers for a ride home with his groceries. His legs hurt terribly and he couldn't make the walk with the grocery sacks.

After Jane put her groceries in the car, she noticed this same man standing outside the store with his groceries. Jane felt prompted to offer him a ride.

So she approached him asking him if he needed a ride. The man said he wasn't supposed to ask women for rides. But Jane responded, "You didn't ask me, I asked you," and he accepted. On the way home Jane learned the man was a retired factory worker and that his first name was Ralph.

When she got him home she helped carry the groceries upstairs to his second-floor apartment. He explained to her that he was living on $414 a month and that the $4 cab ride would have to come out of his $18 a week grocery budget.

Jane was so touched by this kind man's need that she began shopping every Friday at the same store and suggested they ride together each week. Finally one week she called him on Thursday to see if he wanted to shop together the next day. He did . . . and they shopped together each Friday after that. Eventually their trips included lunch.

After several months, Ralph decided to tell Jane more about himself. He stumbled about and then said very directly: "I'm on parole for child molestation." He then told her of his conviction and jail time for his offense.

At that moment the painful experiences of Jane's child abuse flashed through her mind. But surprisingly, instead of feeling hatred toward him, as she had harbored toward her parents for years, she felt a new desire to forgive them all. Suddenly the last step of her recovery program was complete. Now she could help others get free.

Obey the prompting of the Holy Spirit on behalf of others. The answer to your own prayer may be in helping others.

*For if you forgive men when they sin against you, your heavenly Father will also forgive you.* — Matthew 6:14 (NIV)

She boarded the bus looking ragged and threadbare, her wrinkled sunken face showing the stress of her years. She wore a dirty shirt and worn out jeans, both damp from the chilly rain. Her dark hair was matted and stuck out in points. She carried a tattered quilt — tied at the corners to hold her laundry — and an open purse in which she was carrying a head of cabbage. And she was obviously drunk.

As the bus started forward the motion forced her down hard onto a man's lap. Mumbling, she moved to an empty seat, then began searching for her bus fare. As she did, her cabbage escaped and rolled down the aisle. Once she retrieved it she was able to resume the search of her cumbersome purse.

At last the bus reached her stop and she stood to exit. "You haven't paid your fare," said the bus driver kindly. "Yes, I know," she replied. "Please allow me," broke in Sally, a fellow passenger, while stepping forward to pay her fare. The tipsy woman nodded in a dazed acknowledgment then staggered off the bus. Once outside, the woman's quilt broke open and her laundry tumbled into the wet gutter. For a moment, she stood quietly holding one end of the quilt —

unable to fully comprehend what had happened. Then, as the bus pulled away, she sat on the bench near the curb and began to desperately weep.

"Stop!" Sally yelled, and the bus driver slowed to a halt. Though miles from her stop, Sally bolted from the bus to the spot where the woman sat. For a second, she stood poised to begin picking up laundry. Then, instead, she sat down next to the woman, placed her arms around her, and leaned her head against the woman's matted hair. "Jesus loves you and I love you," was all she said.

Years later, a grandmother celebrated Christmas with two grandchildren she hadn't even known were born when she sat at the bus stop that day. It was the woman, now fruitful in service in her local church downtown. She had also worked a part time job selling fruit in the open market for eight years. This year, as usual, when the woman celebrated the birth of her Savior, she also gave thanks for His handmaiden, Sally, who had shared His love and changed her life so many years ago.

Be compassionate toward those who are down and out. People you know may be only one paycheck away from homelessness.

*The Spirit of the Lord is upon me, because he has anointed me to preach the gospel to the poor.* — Luke 4:18 (NIV)

# Community
## *Little Unexpected Touches*

Help your child organize a community trash pickup day with her friends. You provide adult supervision, trash bags and plastic gloves. Over "victory" snacks, have each child compose and sign a letter to the mayor thanking him or her for their service and telling the official how the children are participating in community service.

Give a new neighbor a "coupon book of favors" that you will provide as she needs. You might include *Tea and Conversation, A Lift Within a 10-Mile Radius, A Bundle of Flowers or Herbs from My Garden*, and *A Week of Newspaper and Mail Pickup When You're Out of Town.*

Volunteer to deliver meals to elderly shut-ins once a month.

Dress as a clown and visit a children's hospital. Give each child a flower to remind him that God made us and He can "fix" us.

# *Community*
## *Little Unexpected Touches*

Keep a packet of fast-food gift coupons in your purse or pocket for the hungry or homeless who cross your path.

Put money in the parking meter of the car next to yours if it has run out of time.

Have your children create some special "art" for an elderly shut-in friend and let them deliver it — maybe with a song!

Offer to swap seats to allow passengers traveling together to sit together on the plane, train, or bus.

Take a cake or casserole to a neighbor that you know has a special need — perhaps one who is grieving the loss of a loved one, just home from the hospital, or entertaining unexpected company.

Welcome new neighbors with a small basket of muffins or home-made cookies, and a half-gallon of cold milk and paper cups, while they are "moving in."

# *Community*
## *Little Unexpected Touches*

Rake the leaves that fall from your trees out of your neighbors' yards.

Give one morning a month to helping out at a
shelter for the homeless.

Send thank-you cards during the holiday season to your local fire and
police station, thanking these civil servants for the work they do on
your behalf.

Is there a congregation member in your church who hasn't been there
for a while who would attend if you picked him or her up? If so . . .
offer a ride!

What happens to the flowers that adorn your church altar or pulpit
area after Sunday services are finished? Consider turning them into
smaller bouquets to take to parishioners
who are homebound or hospitalized!

# Community
## *Little Unexpected Touches*

When visiting a sick friend in the hospital, take along a second bouquet of flowers for the stranger in the other bed, or for a person in a nearby room.

Each time you purchase canned goods, buy an extra can or two and put them in a special sack in your pantry, closet, or garage. That way, when the call goes out for "food drives," you'll be prepared!

Pray your way through your church directory or your local phone book, praying for three or four families or individuals a day as part of your daily prayer time.

Write a note of encouragement once a month to an elected official.

If a neighbor is out of town, pick up the hand-delivered circulars that are left unattended at the front door.

Mow the grass or clean house for someone who is ill.

# *Community*
## *Little Unexpected Touches*

Start a drive to build a playground for children in a low-income, apartment complex who do not otherwise have access to a safe backyard.

Make your home a "safety zone" for neighborhood children who may be in some kind of danger.

If your child's team wins the championship, suggest that the winners treat the losers to a pizza party.

To promote interdenominational harmony, organize a charity meal such as a spaghetti supper—cooked and served by members of the various congregations and earmark the proceeds for a local food bank.

Ask your family and a few friends to join you in "adopting" a stretch of highway (with your town's okay). Spend part of one day each month clearing the shoulders and median of litter.

# *Community*
## *Little Unexpected Touches*

Keep your yard clean and your home's exterior in good repair; it can be your gift to the neighborhood.

Be a volunteer worker for a politician you believe in. (And pray for those you don't!) And above all, VOTE!

Throw a "Christmas in July" party. Have each guest bring a warm-weather gift for residents of a local homeless shelter.

When you finish reading your favorite magazines, leave them in the laundry room in your apartment complex, or in your local laundromat, for someone else to enjoy.

During daylight hours, park at the far end of a shopping center lot to leave the closer spaces for someone who might need them more.

# Community
## *Little Unexpected Touches*

Each year on your birthday, make a donation (money, goods, or service) to a place that helped make you the person you are today such as your church, school, library, museum, sports organization, girls' or boys' club.

Do you like to put bumper stickers on your car? Be sure to choose ones that are uplifting in some way — and drive like you mean what they say!  The same goes for T-shirts with messages. Keep them positive; don't incite a riot.

Be there for others. Cheer on Little League teams, salute marching bands in local parades, applaud at dance recitals and encourage runners in races. Just because you don't know the participants, doesn't mean you can't say, "Good job!"

Write a letter to the editor of your local paper to praise someone in city government who kept a promise.

# *Community*
## *Little Unexpected Touches*

Check with your local hospital to see if volunteers are needed to spend time in the children's ward — to play games, read stories, talk, or just hold a hand and calm some fears. Arrange to visit on a regular basis.

Take a small plastic bag with you when you go for walks. Use it to pick up any litter you see.

Concerned about safety in your neighborhood? Ask the police department to send an officer to your home to discuss ways to prevent crime. Invite your neighbors.

Take a Red Cross course to learn basic first-aid techniques, artificial resuscitation, and cardiopulmonary resuscitation (CPR). You never know when you might need those skills to help a person in need.

When you see a disabled car on the side of the road with people in it, call the Highway Patrol, just in case they haven't been able to call for help.

# Community
## *Little Unexpected Touches*

Be a quiet neighbor. Try to keep the stereo, the kids and the dog on low volume. Mow the lawn at a time of day when it's less likely to wake people up.

Keep the shrubs at the edge of your property well trimmed. Make it easier for your neighbors to see traffic, people walking down the sidewalk and bicycle riders.

Get up early one morning to thank your newspaper carrier for a job well done.

At Christmas time, suggest to your children that each one buy or make one gift for a less fortunate child. You can find the name of such a child through a local charity or the Salvation Army.

P.O. Box 55388
Tulsa, Oklahoma 74155